MORE
Wit & Wisdom of

ONLY FOOLS
and
HORSES

D1470876

Splendid
BOOKS

MORE
Wit & Wisdom of
ONLY FOOLS
★★★ and ★★★
HORSES

Compiled by Dan Sullivan

Foreword by Nicholas Lyndhurst

Splendid
BOOKS

Only Fools and Horses was created and written by John Sullivan OBE

This book published in 2013 by Splendid Books Limited

Copyright © 2013 Dan Sullivan / Shazam Productions Limited
www.shazamtv.com

The right of Dan Sullivan to be identified as the Author of the work has been asserted in accordance with the Copyright, Designs and Patents Act 1988.

Only Fools and Horses format and television scripts
© John Sullivan/Shazam Productions Limited

Splendid Books Limited
The Old Hambledon Racecourse Centre
Sheardley Lane
Droxford
Hampshire
SO32 3QY
United Kingdom

www.splendidbooks.co.uk

British Library Cataloguing in Publication Data is available from The British Library.

978-1-909109-01-8

Consultant Editor: Jim Sullivan
Commissioning Editors: Steve Clark and Shoba Vazirani

Designed by Swerve Creative
www.swerve-creative.co.uk

Printed and Bound in the United Kingdom

Every effort has been made to fulfil requirements with regard to reproducing copyright material. The publisher will be glad to rectify any omissions at the earliest opportunity.

Photographs: Radio Times (jacket)
Scope Features (pages 11, 17, 25, 43, 57, 63, 71, 91, 97)   Mirrorpix (page 53)

CONTENTS

FOREWORD BY
NICHOLAS LYNDHURST

An actor's career is 90 per cent luck. John Sullivan suggested me for a role in Only Fools and Horses because he'd seen me in a show called Going Straight. I'd had a tiny role, maybe three lines an episode, but John remembered me. That was my first bit of luck. Then, the first and second choice of actors to play Del weren't available. David Jason was – the second bit of luck.

The following 23 years I would describe as quite a ride. The show began with very poor ratings. There was almost a national disinterest in it. I couldn't understand why our writer, a shy and unassuming man, wasn't getting the credit he deserved. After all, this was funny stuff right? We needn't have worried. Jump forward a couple of years and the merest glimpse of a little yellow three-wheeled-van on location meant crowds of people sometimes hanging around for hours just to watch what "those two" would be up to next. The nation had taken Only Fools to its heart.

So began a wonderful routine of dusty rehearsal rooms, technical runs, re-writes, studio days, audiences queuing outside the television centre, blind terror and, of course, huge laughs. And what laughs they were... sometimes I thought I'd never breathe in again. But always in the background, watching us perform, pencil in one hand and packet of fags in the other, stood John Sullivan. He'd be quietly nodding his head, faintly grinning and so very proud.

I have so many wonderful memories of my time on Fools - details of the practical jokes the cast played on each other alone would fill another three pages. Of course there were pressures. Going from 30 minutes to 50 meant almost twice the work in the same amount of rehearsal time (seven days) and at one stage as the country settled down to watch episode one of series six we were in the studio recording episode two! That's tight.

I'm often asked which is my favourite episode. The short answer is all of them, but two episodes from a very early series stick in my mind. The first is A Touch of Glass, universally known as the chandelier one and the second is The Russians are Coming. The latter not because of any great visual gag, but because of a hugely touching page of dialogue delivered by Lennard Pearce recalling Grandad's reaction to soldiers coming home during the First World War. It made me cry – and sitcoms aren't supposed to make you cry, unless they are written by John Sullivan.

Filming for so many years in so many locations obviously brings about some funny stories (some are unrepeatable!) but a moment very early on in the filming of series one has always stuck in my mind. We were in London's Chapel Street Market. It was early morning. The sky was black and the rain coming down in buckets. The cast and crew were sheltering under huge umbrellas. We were cold and bored. Into this rather bleak scenario a schoolgirl aged about seven or eight came running, soaked to the skin and looking for shelter. There was a huge clap of thunder and she dived under the brolly I had been given. I watched her as she caught her breath, her puzzled face trying to make sense of what she could see - a large group of grown men and women trying to shelter from awful weather in an otherwise deserted street.

"What you all doing mister?" she said.

"We're making a TV programme," I replied.

"What's it called?"

"It's called Only Fools and Horses..."

She considered this for a moment, looked again at the drenched and morose group of filmmakers and said..."Where are the horses then?"

I will always be very grateful that I was chosen

11

to be a part of such an iconic television show. Fools and I grew up together and it's lovely when people say to me: 'I watched it with my father, now I watch it with my son' but for me, the most enduring memories are of John Sullivan, our quiet genius. I was able to count him as a friend and that makes me the luckiest actor there is.

Nicholas Lyndhurst

ART, CULTURE,
FASHION AND
HISTORY

Putting me in a pair of green wellies will not turn me into Archduke Ferdinand. I will be Rodney Trotter in a pair of green wellies - **Rodney**

The only times my clothes look fashionable is when I'm watching UK Gold - **Raquel**

You stick me in front of the telly with a Singapore Sling, a ham sandwich and a bit of Chekhov and I'm as happy as a sand boy - **Del**

"Del on Miranda: She's very impressed. She knows I know a lot about antiques, don't she?
Rodney: Oh yeah. Well, you've been out with a few, ain't yer?"

15

How can I change the lywics to 'Cwying'? The bloody song's called 'Cwying'! - **Tony Angelino**

"Miranda: Do you like Cezanne?
Del: Oh yeah; a bit of ice and lemonade, it's lovely.**"**

"Denzil: That's Derek Trotter in there, not bloody Einstein!

Trigger: Del knows what he's talking about and I don't see what the Beatles' manager's got to do with it, anyway.**"**

I heard that she was the one that cut the ribbon on the opening of Stonehenge - **Del on Elsie Partridge**

We gave you the world's greatest sailors, pal. Remember that. We gave you Nelson, we gave you Drake, we gave you Columbus – **Del to an American**

There is a Rhino Loose in the City – **Del**

Del, thanks to your high profile, we now have a company called 'TIT' and a director with 'DIC' after his name - **Rodney**

He helps me and I help him. It's 'conseil d'etat' as they say in Grenobles - **Del**

They stopped making spares for that van years ago. I've tried everywhere. Breaker's yards, spares shops, archaeologists... - **Rodney**

Del, these dolls ain't called Barbie or Cindy. These dolls are called Lusty Linda and Erotic Estelle - **Rodney**

He's the sort of bloke, if he had a flower shop, right, he'd close on St Valentine's day - **Del on Rodney**

As it happens, I know this little bloke down in Wapping, he'll fix you up a treat. He's Iranian but he has got contacts in Persia - **Del**

Now, all this equipment here, is manufactured by the one country that leads the world in Alpine clothing, namely Fiji - **Del**

These canteens of cutlery are a very exclusive line. You can only buy these at Harrods, Liberty's and Patel's Multimart – **Del**

With your diploma and my yuppy image, we're on the way up – **Del to Rodney**

Look, I spend half my life trying to hide my business deals. The last thing I need is to have 'em all recorded on a floppy bloody disc - **Mike**

This is sonic, state of the art technology, this. And this is none of your Japanese or your German rubbish, no sir, this is actually made in Albania – **Del**

Enjoy ourselves? Del, we are two thousand pounds in debt, we have a garage load of hooky doors and a mob of irate Rastafarians after our blood – **Rodney**

I don't believe what he's doing to me. Here I am, on the verge of losing the biggest deal of my life and this plonker here wants to give me a lecture on poxy butterflies - **Del on Rodney**

EDUCATION
AND RELIGION

"Mickey Pearce: I've just come from evening school. I'm learning Aikido.
Del: Really? Go on then, say something."

Del, you can't speak French. You're still struggling with English - **Rodney**

I've got a GCE in maths and art. I ain't got a GCE in pork - **Rodney**

29

You've always been the same, even when you was at school, nothing but books, learning, education... That's why you're no good at snooker – **Del to Rodney**

"Albert: He's been missing for twelve hours. Twelve hours, that's nearly half a day.
Rodney: I know, I've got a GCE in maths, haven't I?"

"Del: I have come to confess my sins.
Priest: Del, please. I've been invited out
to dinner this evening."

Our Mum was a wonderful woman. She had long golden, blonde hair... sometimes – **Del to Rodney**

It's a good thing your Mum died when she did 'cause that would've killed her – **Grandad to Del**

Me and your Aunt Ada didn't talk to each other for years but she was still my wife - **Albert**

I do remember... sort of, but it's misty... This blonde lady and... she was there and then she wasn't. Bit like the SDP really - **Rodney on his Mum**

I don't believe this conversation. In 35 seconds, you two have married me, buried me and given me widow skin trouble - **Rodney**

"Trigger: Did you ever meet my Nan?
Rodney: Well, only at her funeral.**"**

That bloke has been in shark infested seas, he's been attacked by Kamikaze pilots and blown up more times than a beach ball - **Del on Albert**

If that Freddie the Frog was going out with a married woman on this estate, why did he leave all his money to our Mum? - **Del**

She knew who my Dad was... roughly –
Trigger on his Mum

He may be perverted but he's not dangerous –
Del on Rodney

"Albert: When I came to live with you two, I hoped that I'd end my days here.
Rodney: Yeah, so did we.**"**

"Albert: D'you know what'd look good on you, Rodney? A big white Stetson.
Rodney: D'you know what'd look good on you, Albert? A Dobermann pinscher!**"**

Michael Jackson's got Bubbles, I've got Rodney
- **Del**

"**Rodney:** Well, if I've always been such
a let-down, why did you insist on having
me around?
Del: To keep my promise to Mum… and
you never know when you might need
some bone marrow."

I do not believe what that garrity old git has done to us. I mean, the only hole he hasn't fallen down is the black one in Calcutta – **Del on Albert**

My Mum was a lady. D'you know, she was the first woman in Peckham to smoke menthol cigarettes? – **Del**

Del's gotta be the only bloke who can buy a gold identity bracelet and take it to a dyslexic engraver - **Rodney**

"Grandad on Mickey Pearce: He'd rob his own grandmother, he would.
Rodney: Oh, don't be stupid Grandad… that was never proved."

Stone me, Rodney! We see more of Hayley's Comet than we do of him – **Del on his father**

"Chief Robson: Have you any idea what a 'Psycho' as you so eloquently put it, is?

Grandad: 'Course I have. It's a geezer what dresses up in his mother's clothes."

Look, understand one thing Cass, I am not getting like Del. No way Pedro! - **Rodney**

Last week, we was having a row about who's turn it was to go down the chippy and you claimed that Mum said, on her deathbed, 'send Rodney for the fish' - **Rodney to Del**

Take no notice of him. He's an old sailor. He's still got a bit of depth charge lodged in his brain – **Del on Albert**

They reckon when he boarded his last ship, the crew shot an Albatross for luck – **Rodney on Albert**

"Grandad: Del Boy, I'd like to be cremated.
Del: Well, you'll have to wait 'til the morning, 'cause they'll be closed now."

"Slater: Is this your Grandad?
Del: No, that's the au pair, innit?"

You should come round to Trotter Towers with me one morning, Cass. It'd give Terry Waite the shakes. You can't move for teething rings, Farley's rusks and funny smells. It's like Nightmare on Sesame Street - **Rodney**

"Albert: Del wouldn't mind if I borrowed some of his after shave, would he?
Rodney: What d'you wanna use after shave for? You've got Epping bloody Forest growing out of your chin."

It's like my dear old Mum used to say 'There's none so blind as them what won't listen' – **Del**

When you get to twenty and your six-year-old brother is taller than you are, it makes you think, dunnit? – **Del**

You're not interested, Rodney, are yer? So it's purely epidemic innit, eh? – **Del**

"**Rodney:** I'm just seeing my mates, that's all.
Del: Yeah but why are they always the same mates, eh? Johnnie Walker and Ron Bacardi?"

FOOD
AND DRINK

Food is for wimps - **Del**

He was a bit confused when he came in the other night. Confused as a newt – **Albert on Rodney**

All I asked you to do was put the box of wine in the fridge and me tub of Neapolitan ice cream in the freezer, but no, you get that arse about face, don't yer? So come nine o'clock all I could offer her was a bowl of gunge and a Beaujolais ice lolly – **Del to Grandad**

No, no Rodney. I'll get the sandwiches 'cause you bought the Rolls - **Del**

Seems like nothing's gonna change my luck. Raquel says we ought to try Feng Shui. I said to her 'what good is eating raw fish gonna do?' - **Del**

Come on, let's go down to Sid's cafe. Whenever we reach historic moments like this, I feel like a fry up - **Del**

If a nightingale sang, now, in Berkeley Square, someone would eat it - **Del**

Michael, Michael! Please, a bottle of Champagne for my partner and me... and make it the best Champagne, a bottle of that Dillinger's '75 – **Del**

I'm a caviar person, me, you know... most probably – **Del**

"Del: One of my most favouritest meals is Duck a L'Orange, but I don't know how to say that in French.
Rodney: It's canard.
Del: You can say that again bruv."

★ ★ ★

That curry's doing a conga in my colon –
Boycie, on having eaten Del's
homemade 'Chicken Trotter' curry.

"Corrine on Del: Denzil, how can you trust this man? Every time you meet him you end up drunk or out of pocket.
Denzil: Yeah I know, but he's a mate."

The only time you ever made women jealous was the night you won the last house at bingo - **Del to Mickey Pearce**

That bloke's been on the dole for so long, they invite him to the staff dance - **Del on Mickey Pearce**

Come on Roy, you didn't lose your friends... you didn't have any to lose in the first place - **Del to Slater**

He's everywhere I go, you know. He's on the phone to me, he's at my front door, he's in the betting shop, he's in the pub and now he's in the bloody traffic jam. You know what, Rodney, I get this feeling he's haunting me, know what I mean?
– **Denzil on Del**

Well, this has been nice, like old school days. You and me sat at the same desk… only this time you didn't put frog spawn in my milk – **Slater to Del**

"Trigger: When we was at school Del was the best in our class at chemistry. He used to sell homemade fireworks. He even blew up the science lab once.
Denzil: Yes, I remember. I was doing detention in there at the time."

"Albert: Rodney, innit?
Rodney: Well, it is when Trigger ain't about, yeah."

"Del: ICI have dropped a point.
Rodney: Yeah? Chelsea dropped three on Saturday."

It sort of burnt me right across the forehead here. The bloke who sold it to me said it was a hairdryer. It turns out to be an electric paint stripper –
Mike to a doctor in A & E.

"Denzil: For all we know he could be part of Al-Qaeda!
Del: Does he look like he works in a furniture store?**"**

Ten years from now, I won't be able to raise a smile, let alone anything else - **Del**

D'you realise, if all my veins and arteries were stretched out in a line, they'd circle the world twice? - **Albert**

She could be sitting out there with a belly full of people. One hot bath and we could get chucked out for overcrowding - **Del**

"Rodney: She's most probably at the right temperature.
Del: Stone me, Rodney! What are you two trying for, a baby or a barbecue?"

"Miss McKenzie: Actually, when I left school, I wanted to be a choreographer.
Del: Did you really? What a coincidence, 'cause I always wanted to go into the medical profession myself."

A year ago, you and Cassandra were really trying for this baby, weren't ya? I mean you was at it like a pair of goats. I remember that you became so pale, you had to have your passport photo redone - **Del to Rodney**

I remember the night that Damien was born. It was a wonderful, wonderful moment. But it was very, very traumatic and very, very stressful. But it wasn't a walk in the park for you, Raquel, was it, either? – **Del**

I know you don't want to have an operation. Nobody wants to have an operation but everyone, at some time in their lives, has to have one and today it's your turn – **Del to Albert**

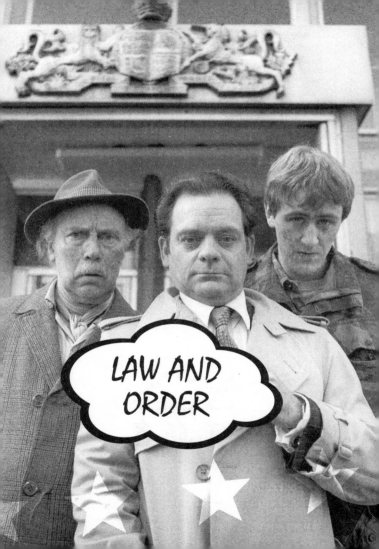

"**Grandad:** He's got a police record.
Del: Yeah, it's 'Walking on the Moon'."

It's lucky you're not a judge, Rodney. You'd hang 'em before they finished the oath - **Grandad**

"Del: Well Boycie, I hope you won't take offence by what I'm about to say but me and Rodney think you've murdered Marlene and buried her in the garden.

Boycie: How dare you! Murdered my wife and buried her in the garden? I've never been so insulted in all my life. You know how much I've spent on that garden, you think I'm gonna dig a hole in it?**"**

"Slater: I heard a whisper that you're flogging pirate tapes.
Boycie: Yeah... Treasure Island, Mutiny on the Bounty..."

I ain't ever been to Rampton. Who started them rumours about me being in Rampton? I ain't ever been to Rampton! I've been to Broadmoor once or twice but that's beside the point - **Mental Mickey**

"Mickey Pearce: I had a fight with five blokes last night.
Del: What was it, a pillow fight?"

I have a good mind to report your beard to the council - **Del to Albert**

"Rodney: Everywhere I went the walls would be whispering 'Beast...... beast'. There'd be posses of 'em waiting for me in the shower room, there'd be razors in my soap, there'd be broken glass in my porridge...

Grandad: Oh, you'd soon learn to adapt, Rodney."

I had no choice. If there had been a way of avoiding it, I would have, but his rear light was defective... I mean what else could I do? - **Slater on arresting his own father**

He's got more grasses than Fisons - **Del on Slater**

Oh, they're smashing blokes, Unc. It's like bumping into the Two Ronnies, Biggs and Kray – **Rodney on the Driscoll Brothers**

They seek him here, they seek him there, those policemen seek him everywhere. Is he in heaven? Is he in hell? That damn elusive sha-a-dow – **Lennox Gilbey aka The Shadow**

"Trigger: There's nothing to be nervous about, Denzil. All you've got to do is go in there and tell the truth.

Denzil: Trig, if I go in there and tell the truth, Del and Rodney are going to be spending the next five years, sharpening Jeffrey Archer's pencils.**"**

"Rodney: Wherever I lay my hat, that's my home.
That's the sort of guy I am.
Trigger: Yeah? You got a hat then now have you, Dave?"

It'll all be 'Rez de Chaussee' as they say in the Doudogne – **Del**

Women are from Venus, men are from Peckham – **Raquel**

'Après moi la deluge' as they say in the
Latin Quarter - **Del**

"Rodney: I'd heard that because of the
precarious state of the world,
Boycie and Marlene had decided
against starting a family.
Vicar: Oh really? I'd heard Boycie
was a Jaffa.**"**

Everything's alright Rodney. I mean, we've got no money, no business and our future's about as bright as a Yugoslavian tour operator's, but no, everything's cushty! - **Del**

"I'll be back". He always says that. D'you know what his nickname is? The Turbanator – **Del on Dr Singh.**

I am, as the French say 'oeufs sur le plat' - **Del**

My old man let me down when he walked out and left me to fend for myself. Then my Mum died, that weren't her fault but I felt she'd let me down. It's funny the things that go through your head when you're sixteen and all alone. I think that's why I've always been straight and upfront with people - **Del**

92

"Del: Alright, so I might occasionally tell the odd porky or two, but I'll tell ya something I don't do. I don't go around pubs dressed in stockings and suspenders, flashing my boobs at geezers, do I Rodney?

Rodney: No, he's never done anything like that."

LOVELY JUBBLY

The stars? You don't need to read your horoscope, Rodney, to realise you're in dead lumber - **Del**

"Rodney: I ain't laughing. I ain't laughing today, I ain't laughing tomorrow… I don't wanna laugh for the rest of my life.
Albert: Well, as long as you're happy, son.**"**

I don't believe this! The one job in the paper I really fancied, and it's mine! – **Rodney**

No, that's stimulated fur, that – **Del on Raquel's new 'fur' coat.**

He's been down more holes than Tony Jacklin –
Del on Albert

"Albert: It's not fair.
Del: Nor is Frank Bruno's arse but he
don't go on about it!"

LOVE AND
ROMANCE

I've got so many things worrying me. You know, I mean, the Polar Cap is melting, the continental shelves are shifting, the rain forest is dying, the sea is being poisoned... and I ain't had a bit for months – **Rodney**

Linda, nice girl. Had a funny eye. Never knew if she was looking at me or seeing if the bus was coming - **Trigger**

I don't want you lumbering me with some old bow wow who don't know the difference between a Liebfraumilch and a can of Tizer - **Del**

"Rodney: I said 'don't play with me girl, 'cause you are playing with fire'. I said 'don't you dare try to tie me down'.
Trigger: She's into all that, is she?"

"Del: When she walks in she... well, she lights up a room.
Rodney: Yeah. Most of your birds walk in and light up a fag.**"**

Rodney, you came storming in just at the moment when I was asking Raquel if she would be kind enough to consider stamping my card - **Del**

The last time you went out with a bird, you took her to a Bay City Rollers concert - **Rodney to Mickey Pearce**

"**Del:** Me and Junie broke up about nineteen and a half years ago, right, that means she was expecting her at the time, which means Debbie is my kid.
Trigger: But she's a pretty girl."

Derek, will you get it into your thick skull, I'm not trying to meet intelligent and sensitive people. I'm happy with you - **Raquel**

It's alright, Raquel. You don't have to be frightened of the Great Raymondo no more. Del Boy is here - **Del**

"Albert on Rodney's new girlfriend: He told me she looked like Crystal Carrington.
Del: Crystal Carrington? Crystal bleedin' Palace more like."

LOVELY JUBBLY

Come on, Marlene. Let's go home and ignore each other for the evening - **Boycie**

"June: Debbie won't be a minute. She's just putting some clothes on.
Rodney: Oh, she needn't bother.**"**

She was a beautiful woman, a bit like Ginger Rogers. The last time I saw her, she looked more like Fred Astaire - **Albert on his wife**

I started thinking about some of the birds that I knocked about with and, cor blimey Rodney, some of 'em have been round the track more times than a lurcher - **Del**

Christmas was approaching, Del asked me what I'd like. 'Anything you want sweetheart, just name it'. So, I said I wouldn't mind a little number by Bruce Oldfield... He got me Tubular Bells -
Raquel

"Del: The old 'uns are the best 'uns, Rodney.
Rodney: No, we're talking about boats now, Del, not your birds."

You get on the blower and give Raquel the old S.P. Oh, and tell her to keep on her toes 'cause the last girl I met at Waterloo Station got mugged on the escalator - **Del**

I'm fed up having to defend you. The times I've said to 'em 'Yes, he's ugly but he's successful' – **Marlene to Boycie**

Girls always blow him out after a couple of weeks. That boy's been blown out more times than a windsock – **Del on Rodney**

You don't know what it's like to have a wife who can't have children. I've tried to console her. I've said 'Marlene, God didn't mean you to have kids so shut up about it.' - **Boycie**

"Rodney on his new girlfriend:
D'you know who she looks like? She looks like that Linda Evans out of Dynasty.
Albert: Which one's that, Joan Collins?"

This wonderful land of ours is on the eve of a golden age of the black market... and you and me, we're gonna be in there first - **Del to Rodney**

"Del: Rodney, I know you may find this hard to believe… and it might even come as a bit of a shock to ya… we are millionaires.

Rodney: Oh good. Perhaps we can take that magnet off the electricity meter now."

We owe two months rent, we are drinking tea with no milk in it and the Electricity Board keep calling round to see why their meter is running backwards – **Rodney**

I'm down that casino every night 'til the early hours of the morning, trying to win us some money. If she knew how much I owed 'em, she'd realise how hard I've been trying – **Del**

In the words of General MacArthur, 'I will be back, soon'... I'm not leaving our birthright down there in Davy Smith's locker, no way – **Del on discovering Freddie the Frog's gold was buried at sea**

If Elsie Partridge really could raise the dead then half the money lenders in Peckham would be employing her - **Boycie**

A couple of years ago, right, some guru reckoned
the world would end within a month and Danny
Driscoll bet a grand that it would... and he's the
brains of the outfit – **Del**

"Del: You'll be in the market place, right, and you'll be selling. I'll be up there in the factories and the warehouses and I'll be buying. And if you find the line is going particularly well all you've gotta do is get on the blower to me, y'see, and you say 'Del Boy, buy, buy, buy!'

Rodney: Yeah! And then you can get on the blower to me and say 'sell, sell, sell!'"

"Rodney: I've only got twenty quid on me.
Del: What happened to your wages?
Rodney: This is my wages."

I've got so many of his slates under here, I could retile the bloody roof – **Mike on Del**

You look as though you've just come back from a Club 18-30 trip to Chernobyl – **Del to Rodney**

All those romantic places that you've only heard about in fairy tales. The Lee Valley viaduct, the glow of Lower Edmonton at dusk, the excitement of a walkabout in Croydon – **Del**

Bonjour Trieste! - **Del**

Rodney, I was up there three hours, three bloody hours! I did loop-the-loop over Dimchurch! There was little kids shouting at me 'there goes a spaceman!' - **Del**

"Albert: It's alright Rodney, nothing to worry about. It's just me lungs. We hit a mine coming back from Normandy... I was trapped for twelve hours in a smoke filled engine room.
Rodney: Well, if it's not one thing, it's another, eh?**"**

I wouldn't come home from New Orleans to see Del. I wouldn't come home from the New Forest to see Del - **Rodney**

You sent me half way around the world. I've been to Amsterdam, I've been to Hull and back! – **Del to Boycie**

Just get me back to Peckham as soon as possible, otherwise I'll be saying 'ay up' and breeding whippets before I'm very much older –
Del to Rodney

"Rodney on Grandad: We could
take him to Lourdes.
Del: Lourdes! He don't even like cricket."

That is Bonnet de Douche, as they say in the
Basque region - **Del**

LOVELY
JUBBLY

"**Mike**: 'Ere, Del. You speak a bit of French, don't ya?
Del: What? Potage bonne femme."

Gary! - **Rashid Mahmoon, AKA Gary**

"Rodney: It's a bit of a mystery all this, innit? It's like something out of one of those Agatha Christie films.
Trigger: Yeah, I used to fancy her."

I saw one of them old five pound notes the other day – **Trigger after Del tells him people are impressed by talk of money**

132

"Rodney: On a cold, rainy night in Peckham, somebody has arranged for you four to be in this room at the same time… and nobody knows who and the most important and frightening aspect of the entire mystery… nobody knows why. Now think hard. Who would do something like that?
Trigger: Jeremy Beadle?"

☆ ☆ ☆

Trigger: If it's a girl, they're calling it 'Sigourney' after an actress and if it's a boy, they're naming it 'Rodney' after Dave.

Trigger: You remember Mike, don't you? He's the water diviner from the Nag's Head.

Trigger: Ain't this coach fitted with a fire distinguisher?

Trigger: I have to attend lectures on modern climactic change, what with global warming and Al Pacino... you just don't know what's gonna happen next.

I don't think you and Del would've won first prize... no. You're alright but Del don't look nothing like Tonto - **Trigger to Rodney on him and Del dressed as Batman and Robin**

"Trigger: I'm gonna live it up a bit; discos, nightclubs, golden beaches, blue skies...
Rodney: Sounds great, Trig, where are you going?
Trigger: Ireland.**"**

"**Boycie:** How can you drink with Slater when that's the man who stitched you up over those knocked off stamps and put you away for eighteen months?! **Trigger:** I know, but when I come out I got an electric blanket and a radio with 'em."

"Trigger: I sometimes think about the future. I don't want to end up a lonely bachelor like my cousin Ronnie. Then again he did always have a strange taste in women.
Denzil: In what way?
Trigger: Well, they were men.**"**

I got a room in a motel. They don't know I ain't got a car - **Trigger**

Only Fools and Horses - The Official Inside Story
By Steve Clark
Foreword by Theo Paphitis

> The definitive history of Only Fools and Horses - Sir David Jason

This book takes us behind the scenes to reveal the secrets of the hit show and is fully authorised by the family of its writer John Sullivan.

This engaging tribute contains interviews with the show's stars and members of the production team, together with rarely seen pictures.

Written by bestselling author Steve Clark, the only writer on set for the filming of *Only Fools and Horses*, *The Green Green Grass* and *Rock & Chips*, this book gives a fascinating and unique insight into this legendary series.
£9.99 (paperback)

The Official Only Fools and Horses Quiz Book
Compiled by Dan Sullivan and Jim Sullivan,
Foreword by John Sullivan

Now you can test your knowledge of the legendary sitcom in *The Official Only Fools and Horses Quiz Book*, which is packed with more than 1,000 brain-teasers about the show.

Plus there's an episode guide and an exclusive foreword by the show's creator and writer John Sullivan, who reveals some of the mystery behind the much-loved series and just how he came up with some of television's most memorable moments.
£7.99 (paperback)

The Wit and Wisdom of Only Fools and Horses
Compiled by Dan Sullivan
Foreword by Sir David Jason

The 'crème de la menthe' of the hilarious one-liners from John Sullivan's *Only Fools and Horses* have been brought together for the first time in *The Wit & Wisdom of Only Fools and Horses*.

All of Del, Rodney, Grandad, Uncle Albert, Boycie, Trigger and the rest of the gang's funniest and most memorable lines are here, making this triffic book a pukka 42-carat gold-plated bargain.
£4.99 (paperback)

The British Television Location Guide
By Steve Clark and Shoba Vazirani

This beautifully illustrated book reveals the settings for dozens of top television shows. From *Downton Abbey* to *Doc Martin* and from *Midsomer Murders* to *Broadchurch*, the book gives details of how you can visit the places you have seen so many times on television. It includes details of the locations for more than 100 television series.
Just £9.99 (full colour paperback)

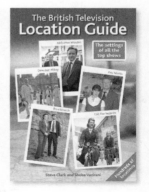

Catching Bullets: Memoirs of a Bond Fan
By Mark O'Connell, Prelude by Barbara Broccoli, Foreword by Mark Gatiss and Afterword by Maud Adams

When Jimmy O'Connell took a job as chauffeur for 007 producers Eon Productions, it would not just be Cubby Broccoli, Roger Moore and Sean Connery he would drive to James Bond. His grandson Mark swiftly hitches a metaphorical ride on a humorous journey of filmic discovery where Bond movies fire like bespoke bullets at a Reagan-era Catholic childhood marked with divorce, a closet-gay adolescence sound-tracked by John Barry and an adult life as a comedy writer still inspired by that Broccoli movie magic.
£7.99 (paperback)

Postcards From A Rock & Roll Tour
By Gordy Marshall, Foreword by Graeme Edge

Postcards From a Rock & Roll Tour is drummer Gordy Marshall's witty and wry take on life on the road touring with legendary rock band *The Moody Blues.*

Part memoir, part travelogue, it's a candid, unexpected and often hilarious account of just what it's like to travel around the world playing to sell-out audiences, living out of a suitcase and spending days and days on a tour bus.

If you thought being in a rock band was all sex, drugs and rock and roll, then think again....
£7.99 (paperback)

FREE
DELIVERY
ON **ALL**
ORDERS

To order:
By phone: **0845 625 3045**
or online: **www.splendidbooks.co.uk**

By post: Send a cheque (payable to Splendid Books Limited) to:
**Splendid Books Limited, The Old Hambledon Racecourse Centre,
Sheardley Lane, Droxford, Hampshire SO32 3QY United Kingdom**

Splendid
BOOKS

Splendid
BOOKS

www.splendidbooks.co.uk

Twitter @splendidbooks
www.facebook.com/splendidbooks

www.facebook.com/onlyfoolsbook
Twitter @onlyfoolsbook